Contents

THE SPECKLED BAND

1

An Early Morning Visitor for Holmes

For many years, I was a good friend of Sherlock Holmes, the famous private detective[1].

During this time, Holmes solved many unusual mysteries. But perhaps one of the most unusual was the mystery of the Speckled Band.

The story began in April, 1883. At that time, Holmes and I were sharing an apartment in Baker Street, in London.

One morning, I woke up very early. To my surprise, Holmes was standing beside my bed. He was already dressed.

'What's happened, Holmes?' I asked. 'Is there a fire?'

'No, Watson,' replied Holmes. 'A client[2] has just arrived. A young lady is waiting downstairs. She seems very worried and upset. I think she has something important to tell me. This could be an interesting case[3], Watson. That's why I woke you up.'

'I'll come at once,' I said.

I was very interested in Holmes' cases. My friend was a very clever detective. I very much admired his work.

So I dressed quickly and went downstairs with Holmes. The lady was waiting in our sitting-room. She was dressed all in black. Over her face she wore a veil[4].

'Good morning, madam,' said Holmes. 'I'm Sherlock Holmes and this is Dr Watson, my friend and helper.' Holmes shut the door and turned to the lady. 'You're shivering, madam,' he said. 'You must be cold. Sit near the fire and I'll get you some hot coffee.'

MACMILLAN READERS

INTERMEDIATE LEVEL

SIR ARTHUR CONAN DOYLE

The Speckled Band
and Other Stories

Retold by Anne Collins

700031433298

MACMILLAN

MACMILLAN READERS

INTERMEDIATE LEVEL

Founding Editor: John Milne

The Macmillan Readers provide a choice of enjoyable reading materials for learners of English. The series is published at six levels – Starter, Beginner, Elementary, Pre-intermediate, Intermediate and Upper.

Level control
Information, structure and vocabulary are controlled to suit the students' ability at each level.

The number of words at each level:

Starter	about 300 basic words
Beginner	about 600 basic words
Elementary	about 1100 basic words
Pre-intermediate	about 1400 basic words
Intermediate	about 1600 basic words
Upper	about 2200 basic words

Vocabulary
Some difficult words and phrases in this book are important for understanding the story. Some of these words are explained in the story and some are shown in the pictures. From Pre-intermediate level upwards, words are marked with a number like this: ...³. These words are explained in the Glossary at the end of the book.

The lady moved nearer the fire. Then she said, 'It isn't the cold which makes me shiver.'

'What is it, then?'

'It's fear, Mr Holmes. It's terror.'

As she spoke, the lady raised her veil. We saw at once that she was very frightened. Her eyes were like the eyes of a terrified animal. She was a young woman, about thirty years old, but her hair was already turning grey with worry.

Holmes looked at the lady carefully. Then he leant forward and touched her arm.

'Don't be afraid,' he said kindly. 'I'm sure we can help you. But first, please tell us your story.'

'Mr Holmes,' said our visitor, 'I know I'm in terrible danger. Please tell me what to do!'

2

Miss Stoner Begins Her Story

'I'm listening carefully,' said Holmes. So the lady began her story.

'My name,' she said, 'is Helen Stoner. My father was an officer in the Indian army. But he died when I was a baby. After his death, my mother, my sister Julia and I continued to live in India. My sister Julia and I were twins[5]. When Julia and I were only two years old, my mother married again. She married a man called Dr Grimesby Roylott. So Dr Roylott became our stepfather.'

'Tell me about Dr Roylott,' said Holmes.

'In the past, Dr Roylott's family were very rich,' said Miss Stoner. 'But, as the years went by, they lost all their money. Now

Dr Roylott has only a large, old house and a small piece of land. The house is called Stoke Moran. I'm living at Stoke Moran with Dr Roylott now.

'When my stepfather was young, he studied medicine. After he became a doctor, he went to India. That's where he met my mother and later married her.

'My mother was a rich woman,' went on Miss Stoner. 'She had a private income[6]. Every year, she received a sum of about one thousand pounds from her bank. When she married Dr Roylott, an agreement was made about this money.'

'What was this agreement?' asked Holmes.

'If my mother died,' replied Miss Stoner, 'Dr Roylott would inherit[7] her income. After her death, he would receive one thousand pounds every year.

'But if my sister or I married, some of the one thousand pounds would go to us instead. We would receive part of the money.'

'I see,' said Holmes.

'After some years, we returned to England from India,' continued Miss Stoner. 'But soon after we got back, my mother was killed in an accident. At first, all our neighbours at Stoke Moran were friendly with my stepfather. They were very happy that someone from the Roylott family was living at Stoke Moran again.

'But my stepfather didn't want to make friends with anyone. Whenever he went out, he quarrelled with somebody. He is a very bad-tempered man and gets angry quickly. Soon, all our neighbours were afraid of him.'

'Didn't he have any friends at all?' asked Holmes.

'His only friends were gypsies[8],' said Miss Stoner. 'These gypsies move round the country in bands[9]. Dr Roylott allows these gypsies to camp on his land.

'Dr Roylott is also very fond of Indian animals. Two of these – a cheetah and a baboon[10] – were sent to him from India. They run around freely over his land. Everyone is terrified of these dangerous animals.

'So Julia and I became more and more unhappy,' went on Miss Stoner. 'No servants wanted to live at Stoke Moran so we had to do all the work. When Julia died . . .'

'Your sister is dead, then?' asked Holmes. At once, he became very interested.

'Yes,' said Miss Stoner. 'She was to be married. The date had been fixed for the wedding. But two weeks before her wedding day, Julia died.'

3

The Death of Julia

Holmes leant forward excitedly.
'Tell me exactly what happened,' he said.

'On the night of Julia's death,' said Miss Stoner, 'my step-father went to his room early. Julia and I were sitting together in my bedroom. We talked until about eleven o'clock. Then Julia went to bed.

'All the bedrooms at Stoke Moran are in the same part of the house. They're all next to each other, on the ground floor.

'The door of each bedroom opens into the same corridor. The windows look out onto the garden. But there are no doors or windows from one bedroom to the next.'

'I understand,' said Holmes.

'As Julia was leaving my room that evening, she asked a strange question.

"Tell me, Helen," she said, "have you ever heard anyone whistle in the middle of the night?"

"No," I said, in surprise. "Why?"

7

"Because, during the past few nights," replied Julia, "I have heard a strange whistle. It's very low and clear. But I don't know where it comes from."

"Remember," I said, some gypsies are camping near the house. Perhaps it was one of them whistling at night."

"You're probably right," Julia replied. "Anyway, it doesn't matter. Goodnight." She smiled at me and closed my door.'

'Did you and Julia always lock your doors at night?' asked Holmes.

'Yes,' replied Miss Stoner. 'We were afraid of the cheetah and the baboon. They're dangerous animals. We didn't feel safe unless our doors and windows were locked.'

'Of course,' said Holmes. 'Please go on.'

'That night, there was a terrible storm,' continued Miss Stoner. 'The wind was howling and the rain was beating on the window. I couldn't sleep. Suddenly I heard a dreadful scream. I knew it was Julia.

'I jumped out of bed and ran into the corridor. As I opened my door, I thought I heard a noise. It was a low, clear whistle. Then I heard another sound. The second sound was like metal clanging against metal.

'I saw that my sister's door was open. I stared at it in horror. Suddenly Julia appeared. She was standing in the doorway. Her face was white with terror. Her eyes were staring wildly. She was swaying from side to side, like a drunk person.

'Then she fell on the floor. Her body moved like someone in terrible pain.

'Suddenly she screamed these words: "Oh, my God! Helen! It was the band! The speckled band!"

'Then she fainted[11]. At that moment, my stepfather came out of his room. He ran down the corridor to help Julia. But there was nothing he could do.

'My stepfather went to the village to bring another doctor. But before he returned, poor Julia was dead.'

'She was swaying from side to side, like a drunk person.'

'How was your sister dressed?' asked Holmes.

'She was wearing her nightdress. In one hand, she was holding a box of matches and, in the other, a burnt match.'

'So she had lit a match to see around her,' said Holmes. 'That could be important. Was the cause of her death ever discovered?'

'No,' replied Miss Stoner. 'Nobody could find out how she died. Her body was not marked in any way. The doors and windows of Julia's room were locked. The chimney was built so that no one could climb down into the fireplace from the roof. Nobody could get in or out of her room. So Julia must have been alone in her bedroom.'

'But what about her strange words – "The speckled band?" ' asked Holmes. 'What do you think she meant?'

'I don't know,' said Miss Stoner. 'But perhaps she meant a band of people. Gypsies were camping near the house. Many of these gypsies wear handkerchiefs[12] on their heads. These handkerchiefs have a design of spots or speckles. So perhaps Julia was trying to describe the band of gypsies.'

Holmes looked doubtful.

'Please go on,' he said.

'Julia died two years ago,' said Miss Stoner. 'Since her death, I've been very lonely. But recently, a dear friend of mine asked me to marry him. We're getting married very soon.

'But two days ago, some builders arrived at Stoke Moran. The builders started to knock a hole through my bedroom wall. So I had to move out of my room and into Julia's room. I've been sleeping in her bed.'

Miss Stoner stopped for a few moments. Then she said, 'Mr Holmes, last night, I heard a terrible sound.'

'What was that?' I asked.

'It was a whistle, Dr Watson. A low, clear whistle. The same sound Julia heard for several nights before she died!'

4

A Dangerous Enemy

Holmes and I looked at each other in astonishment.

'What did you do?' asked Holmes.

'I jumped out of bed and looked around me,' replied Miss Stoner. 'But it was dark and I couldn't see anything. At daylight, I went to the station and caught a train to London. I knew I had to see you, Mr Holmes. You are the only man who can help me.'

'But I can only help you if you tell me everything,' said Holmes. 'you have not told me everything, Miss Stoner.'

'What do you mean?' asked Miss Stoner, in surprise.

Holmes did not answer. He took hold of Miss Stoner's arm and pushed back her sleeve. I saw five red marks on her arm. They were the marks of four fingers and a thumb. Somebody had held Miss Stoner's arm tightly.

'Your stepfather has hurt you badly,' said Holmes. Miss Stoner's face became red.

'Dr Roylott is a very strong man,' she said. 'He doesn't know how strong he is.'

Holmes stared into the fire without speaking. I knew he was thinking hard.

'I need some more information,' he said at last. 'But we must move quickly. I want to go to Stoke Moran today and examine[13] the bedrooms there. But your stepfather must not know about my visit.'

'Dr Roylott has important business in London today,' said Miss Stoner. 'He'll be away from home all day.'

'Excellent!' cried Holmes. 'Will you come with me, Watson?'

'Of course,' I replied.

'Then, Miss Stoner, we'll arrive at Stoke Moran early this afternoon'

'I must go now,' said Miss Stoner. 'But I feel much happier, now that I have told you about my troubles. Goodbye.' She pulled her veil over her face and left the room.

Holmes leant back in his chair.

'Well, Watson,' he said, 'this matter is very strange.'

'I don't understand it,' I said. 'Helen Stoner's sister, Julia, was alone in her bedroom. Nobody could get in or out. So how did she die?'

'And what about the whistle in the night?' said Holmes. 'And the dying woman's words about the "speckled band"?'

'I don't know,' I said. 'Perhaps the band of gypsies . . .'

Suddenly the door of our room was thrown open and a man appeared. He was so large that his body almost filled the doorway. His face was red and his eyes were cruel.

The man stared at Holmes. Then he looked at me.

'Which of you is Holmes?' he asked rudely.

'That's my name,' answered my friend quietly.

'Well, I'm Dr Grimesby Roylott of Stoke Moran,' said the man. 'I know my stepdaughter's been here. I followed her. What has she been saying to you?'

Holmes was not afraid of the large man. He was not going to tell Dr Roylott anything about Helen Stoner's visit. So he said politely, 'The weather is a little cold just now, isn't it?'

'Answer my question!' shouted Dr Roylott angrily. 'What has my stepdaughter been saying to you? I've heard about you, Holmes. You're a busybody. You interfere in other people's lives. Well, keep out of *my* life. I'm a dangerous man. Look!'

A poker was lying beside the fire. It was made of iron and was very heavy. Dr Roylott stepped forward and picked it up. He bent the poker with his huge hands. Then he threw it back into the fireplace.

'I'm warning you, Holmes. Keep out of my life!' he said again. Then he left the room.

Suddenly the door of our room was thrown open and a man appeared.

Holmes began to laugh. 'Well,' he said, 'perhaps I'm not as large as Dr Roylott. But I'm just as strong.'

As he spoke, Holmes picked up the poker and pulled it straight again.

'Now,' said Holmes, 'let's have some breakfast, Watson. Then I have some business to do. I need more information.'

5

A Visit to Stoke Moran

It was nearly one o'clock before Holmes returned. He looked excited.

'I've been to Mrs Roylott's lawyer,' he said. 'I've seen her will[14]. This is what she wanted to happen to her money after her death.

'After her death, Dr Roylott inherited all of his wife's income. But if Julia and Helen Stoner married, they would receive a large part of the income instead.'

'So Dr Roylott would lose a lot of money,' I said.

'Exactly,' said Holmes. 'But now, Watson, we must hurry. And, please, bring your gun with you.'

We caught a train to Leatherhead, the nearest town to Stoke Moran. Then we drove along the country lanes to Dr Roylott's house. It was a beautiful spring day.

Soon we saw a large house through the trees.

'That's Stoke Moran,' said our driver, pointing at the house. 'The quickest way to get there is through the fields. See, where that lady is.'

We saw a lady walking towards us. It was Helen Stoner. We

paid the driver and he set off back to Leatherhead. Miss Stoner hurried forward to meet us.

'We have plenty of time,' she said. 'Dr Roylott won't return from London until this evening.'

'We've already met your stepfather,' said Holmes. He told Miss Stoner about Dr Roylott's visit. Miss Stoner's face went white.

'So he followed me,' she said. 'I'll never be safe from him.'

'Come,' said Holmes. 'Let's examine the bedrooms.'

We walked across the fields to the house. We saw that work was being done on one wall of the house. This was the wall of Miss Stoner's bedroom.

'This is strange,' said Holmes. 'I can't see why this work is necessary.'

'No,' said Miss Stoner. 'I am sure that the work is not necessary. It is an excuse to get me to move from my room.'

'Well,' said Holmes, 'I want to examine the room you're sleeping in now – your sister Julia's room.'

The room was small, with a low ceiling[15] and a wide fireplace. There was some old furniture in the room – a bed, a table and two chairs. Holmes examined everything carefully.

Suddenly he pointed to a long rope which hung down by the bed. The end of this rope touched the pillow. The rope looked like a bell-rope for calling a servant. If the person in bed wanted something, they could pull the rope. The rope would be attached to a bell in another part of the house. The bell would ring and a servant would come.

'That bell-rope looks very new,' Holmes remarked.

'Yes,' replied Miss Stoner. 'It was put in only two years ago.'

Holmes pulled the bell-rope. We waited. But nothing happened. We could not hear a bell ringing anywhere in the house.

'Look,' said Holmes suddenly. 'This isn't a real bell-rope. It doesn't go anywhere. It's attached to a hook on the ceiling.'

Suddenly he pointed to a long rope which hung by the bed.

We all stared up at the ceiling. Holmes was right. Then I noticed something else. Near the top of the bell-rope was a tiny opening in the wall. It looked like a small ventilator. Holmes saw the ventilator too.

'That's strange,' he said. 'Air usually comes into a room from *outside*, through a ventilator. But this ventilator connects two rooms *inside*. I wonder why?'

'I don't know,' said Miss Stoner. 'But the bell-rope and the ventilator were put in at the same time.'

'That's very interesting,' said Holmes. 'A bell-rope which doesn't ring a bell and a ventilator which doesn't ventilate. They are both false. And now, Miss Stoner, I'd like to examine your stepfather's room.'

We went into Dr Roylott's room next door. There were a few pieces of furniture in the room and some books. In the middle of the floor stood a large iron safe[16]. The safe was locked. Holmes knocked on the walls of the safe.

'What's in here?' he asked.

'My stepfather's business papers,' replied Miss Stoner.

'There isn't a cat inside?'

'A cat!' said Miss Stoner, in surprise. 'No. What a strange idea.'

'Well, look,' said Holmes. He pointed to a small saucer of milk on top of the safe.

'We don't have a cat,' said Miss Stoner. 'But there is the cheetah. A cheetah is just a big cat.'

'Yes, of course,' said Holmes. 'But here's something else.'

A short stick was lying on top of the bed. A thin rope was attached to this stick. One end of the rope had been tied into a noose[17]. I looked at the noose. I wondered what it was for.

'Well,' said Holmes. 'I think I've seen enough.'

We walked out into the garden. Holmes looked very serious.

'Miss Stoner,' he said at last, 'Dr Watson and I must wait in your room tonight.'

Miss Stoner and I looked at each other in astonishment.

'Yes,' said Holmes. 'Your life is in great danger.'

6

Dr Roylott Returns

'This is my plan, Miss Stoner,' said Holmes. 'Listen carefully. When Dr Roylott returns, go into Julia's room, but don't go to bed. Wait until you hear Dr Roylott go to bed. Then put a lamp[18] in the window. Then go to your own room. You must stay there all night.

'Dr Watson and I will be watching the house. The lamp in the window will be a signal for us. When we see the lamp, we'll come.'

'But where will you be?' asked Miss Stoner.

Holmes pointed to a building through the trees.

'Is that the village inn[19]?' he asked.

'Yes,' said Miss Stoner.

'Then Dr Watson and I will wait at the village inn,' said Holmes. 'We can watch your bedroom window from there. Goodbye, Miss Stoner, and don't be afraid.'

Holmes and I went to the inn. We paid for a room on the first floor. From our room, we could see Stoke Moran.

As it was getting dark, a horse and carriage came along the road. I saw Dr Roylott sitting in the carriage. The carriage went through the big iron gates at Stoke Moran. Then it drove on, up to the house.

'Watson,' said Holmes, 'we may be in great danger tonight.'

'Why do you think we may be in great danger?' I asked. 'What did you see in those rooms?'

'You remember the bell-rope and the ventilator?'

'Yes,' I said. 'But I don't understand why they are important.'

'Both the bell-rope and the ventilator were put into the room two years ago,' said Holmes. 'But they are false. They don't work. And something else happened two years ago. Julia Stoner died.'

'Yes,' I said. 'But I still don't see . . .'

'Did you notice anything unusual about the bed, Watson?' asked Holmes.

'No.'

'The bed was fixed to the floor. It cannot be moved. It must always stay in the same position – next to the bell-rope and under the ventilator.'

'Holmes!' I cried. 'I'm beginning to understand. The person in the bed cannot escape some terrible danger.'

'Dr Roylott is a very clever man,' said Holmes. 'We're just in time to prevent a horrible crime.'

7

Night of Terror

About eleven o'clock, we saw a light. It was the lamp shining from the bedroom window.

Holmes jumped up excitedly.

'That's our signal, Watson,' he said. 'Come on!'

We hurried along the road. The yellow light was still shining from the bedroom window. We went into the garden of Stoke Moran and walked towards the house.

Suddenly a dark shape ran in front of us. It was like a child with very long arms. But it was not a child. I felt very afraid.

'What was that, Holmes?' I asked.

Holmes laughed quietly.

'It was one of Dr Roylott's animals,' he said. 'That was the baboon.'

We reached the house and climbed through the window, into Julia's bedroom. Holmes closed the window. Then he whispered in my ear.

'We must put out the light, Watson. Dr Roylott might see the light through the ventilator.'

I took my gun out of my pocket and put it on the table. Holmes had brought a long, thin stick with him. He put this stick on the bed. He put a box of matches beside the stick. I put out the lamp and we waited.

I shall never forget that terrible night. We were in complete darkness and we knew we mustn't make a sound. We heard the bell in the village clock. It struck midnight, then one o'clock, two o'clock, three o'clock . . . Still we waited.

Suddenly I saw a light shining through the ventilator. Somebody in Dr Roylott's room had lit a lamp. I heard someone moving about quietly. Then everything was silent again. Another half hour passed.

Then I heard a strange noise – a very soft, hissing noise. The noise was near us in the room. Holmes jumped up and lit a match. Immediately, I heard a low, clear whistle.

Suddenly Holmes began hitting the bell-rope with his stick. By the light of the match, I saw his face. It was full of horror.

'Do you see it, Watson?' he shouted.

But I saw nothing. Holmes stopped hitting the bell-rope and gazed up at the ventilator.

Suddenly we heard a dreadful cry – a cry of pain and terror. I felt cold and sick with fear.

'What was that cry?' I whispered.

'It means that everything is over,' said Holmes. 'Bring your gun and let's go into Dr Roylott's room.'

Holmes lit the lamp. Then I followed him down the corridor to Dr Roylott's room. We knocked twice on the door, but there was no reply. We pushed the door open and entered the room.

A terrible sight met our eyes. Dr Roylott was sitting beside his safe. The door of the safe was open. The short stick with the noose lay across Dr Roylott's knees.

Dr Roylott was dead. His eyes were staring upwards in terror. There was something strange round his head. It was bright yellow, with brown speckles.

'The band,' whispered Holmes. 'The speckled band!'

I stepped forward. Immediately the strange band began to move.

'It's a snake,' I cried in horror.

Quickly Holmes grabbed the stick with the noose on the end. He caught the snake's head in the noose. Then he threw the snake into the iron safe and closed the door. The metal door clanged shut.

8

The Speckled Band

Next morning, we took Helen Stoner away from Stoke Moran. The poor girl was very upset by what had happened. We took her to an aunt's house in London. She would stay there until her wedding.

We also told the police about Dr Roylott's death. Then we returned to our apartment in Baker Street.

'Tell me something, Holmes,' I said. 'How did you know the "speckled band" was a snake?'

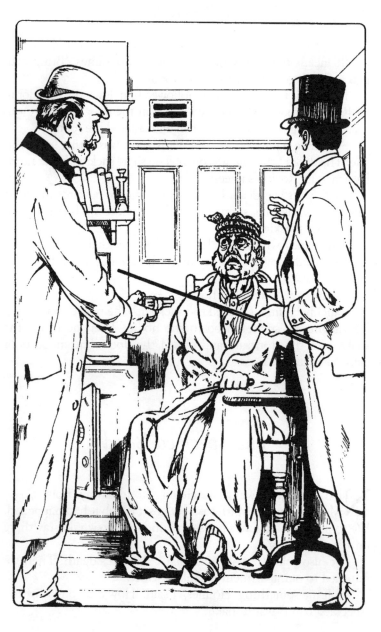

His eyes were staring upwards in terror.

'Well,' said Holmes, 'when I examined Julia Stoner's bedroom, I saw the bell-rope and the ventilator. I saw they were both false. Then I noticed the bed was fixed to the floor.

'And I realised that something could pass through the ventilator. It could travel down the bell-rope and land on the bed. Immediately, I thought of a snake.

'Dr Roylott had other strange animals from India. It would be easy for him to have a snake as well.

'So he kept it in his safe and fed it with milk. And every night he put the snake through the ventilator. It went into his stepdaughter's room and came down the rope. He knew that one night it would bite the girl in the bed.'

'How did he make the snake come back to him?' I asked.

'Dr Roylott's signal to the snake was a whistle,' replied Holmes. 'When the snake heard the whistle, it returned to its master. Julia and Helen Stoner also heard this whistle.'

'On the night her sister died,' I said, 'Helen Stoner heard the sound of metal clanging against metal.'

'That was the safe door clanging shut,' said Holmes.

'So when you heard the hissing noise in the room last night,' I said, 'you knew it was the snake.'

'Yes. So, I hit it with my stick and it went back through the ventilator. But the blows from my stick also made it angry. That's why it bit Dr Roylott.'

'Dr Roylott wanted his stepdaughters' money,' I said. 'He killed Julia Stoner and he tried to kill her sister, Helen, too. But his plans went wrong. The snake finally killed its master.'

'Exactly,' said Holmes. 'And I don't feel very sorry for him.'

THE DANCING MEN

1

A Strange Drawing

One morning, Sherlock Holmes handed me a sheet of paper. 'Look, Watson,' he said. 'Can you explain this problem?'

I looked at the paper. To my surprise, it was covered with a line of strange pictures. These pictures looked like little dancing men.

'A child must have drawn these,' I said. 'Where did you get this piece of paper, Holmes?'

'It arrived by post this morning,' answered Holmes. 'A man called Hilton Cubitt, of Ridling Thorpe Manor in Norfolk, sent it to me. Mr Cubitt is coming to see me today.

'There's a ring at the doorbell, Watson. Perhaps that's Mr Cubitt now.'

A moment later, a tall gentleman entered the room. He had a handsome face with clear blue eyes and looked very strong and healthy.

This gentleman shook hands with both of us. Suddenly he caught sight of the strange drawings.

'Here's a mystery, Mr Holmes,' he said. 'What do you think of these drawings?'

'They look like children's drawings,' replied Holmes. 'But why do you think they are important?'

'I don't, Mr Holmes. But these drawings are making my wife very frightened. That's why I have come to see you. I want to find out what they mean.'

Holmes held up the paper, so that the sunlight shone through it. It was a page torn from a notebook and the markings on it looked like this:

Holmes examined the paper carefully. Then he folded it up and put it in his pocket.

'This is a most interesting and unusual case, Mr Cubitt,' he said. 'Please tell us your story from the beginning.'

2

Mr Cubitt's Story

'I'm not very good at telling stories,' said Mr Cubitt. 'But first, I want to explain something.

'I'm not rich, but I come from a very old and well-known family. My family has lived at Ridling Thorpe Manor, in Norfolk, for nearly five hundred years.

'Last year, while I was visiting London, I met an American lady called Elsie Patrick. Elsie and I became friends and soon fell in love. I didn't know anything about Elsie's family or her past life. But I decided to ask her to marry me.

'The day before our wedding, Elsie spoke to me. "I've had some very sad things happen to me in my past life, Hilton. I've done nothing wrong, but I wish to forget my past. Please promise me you will never ask me anything about it. If you are unable to make this promise, then please go back to Norfolk and leave me."

'So I promised Elsie I would never ask her anything about her past life. We've been married for a year now and we've been very happy. During all this time, I've kept my promise. But one day, about a month ago, my wife received a letter from America – I saw the American stamp. She read the letter and her face turned white. Then she threw the letter in the fire.

'She said nothing, but from that time, there's been a look of fear on her face.

'Mr Holmes, my wife is a very good woman. I'm sure she has not done anything wrong in her past life.

'But Elsie knows I am very proud of my family. My family's long history is very important to me. She would never do anything to upset me. Perhaps that's the reason she's afraid to tell me her troubles.'

'Please go on,' said Holmes.

'Well,' continued Mr Cubitt, 'yesterday morning, a strange thing happened. I found this piece of paper lying on the sundial[20] in the garden. At first, I thought it was a child's drawing.

'But when I showed the paper to Elsie, she fainted. Since then, she has seemed like someone in a dream, and there is terror in her eyes.

'I didn't know what to do. If I took the paper to the police, they would laugh at me. So I came to you. Mr Holmes, please help me. I'm not rich, but I'll spend all my money to protect my wife from danger.'

I was sorry for Mr Cubitt. He was a good man and I saw that he loved his wife very much.

Holmes did not speak for some time.

'Mr Cubitt, don't you think,' he said at last, 'you should ask your wife to tell you everything?'

'But I promised Elsie I would never ask her about her past,' replied Hilton Cubitt. 'If she wants to tell me something, she will. But I will not ask her to tell me.'

'I found this piece of paper lying on the sundial.'

'I'll be pleased to help you,' said Holmes. 'I believe there is a meaning in the pictures of the dancing men. But I need more information before I can say what it is.

'Go back to Norfolk. If there are any more pictures of dancing men, make a copy of them for me. If anything important happens, I'll come to Norfolk at once.'

3

Mr Cubitt's Second Visit

During the next few days, Holmes was very quiet. Several times he looked at the paper with the dancing figures on it.

Then one afternoon, about a fortnight later, we had another visit from Mr Cubitt. He seemed worried and tired.

'My wife hasn't told me anything yet, Mr Holmes,' he said. 'But I have more pictures of dancing men and – more important – I've seen the man who draws them.

'But I'll tell you everything that has happened. The morning after I visited you, I found another line of dancing men. They were drawn with chalk on the toolhouse[21] which stands in the garden, near the house. I made this copy.'

Hilton Cubitt unfolded a paper and laid it on the table.

'Excellent!' cried Holmes. 'Please go on.'

'After I'd made the copy,' continued Mr Cubitt, 'I cleaned

28

off the marks. But two days later, another drawing appeared. Here it is:

Holmes was delighted.

'We're beginning to get a lot of information,' he said.

'I decided to find out who was drawing these pictures,' went on Hilton Cubitt. 'So the next night, I took my gun and sat beside a window which looks out onto the garden.

'At about two o'clock in the morning, my wife came into the room. She was wearing her night clothes. She asked me to come to bed. But I refused.

' "No, Elsie," I said. "I want to see who is drawing these pictures."

'Suddenly I saw Elsie's face turn very white in the moonlight. She was looking out of the window. I looked out of the window, too. I saw something moving near the toolhouse. A dark figure came slowly round the corner of the toolhouse and stopped beside the door.

'Immediately, I picked up my gun. I wanted to run out of the house, but my wife caught me in her arms and held me back. By the time I got outside, the man was gone.

'On the toolhouse door was the same drawing I copied before:

'I looked everywhere, but I couldn't find the man. However, in the morning, when I looked at the toolhouse door again, I saw a second line of dancing men. This new line is very short, but I made a copy and here it is.'

'A dark figure came slowly round the corner of the
toolhouse and stopped beside the door.'

Hilton Cubitt gave another piece of paper to Holmes.

I could see that Holmes was very excited.

'Tell me,' he said, 'was this second line of figures separate from the first?'

'It was on a different part of the door.'

'Excellent!' cried Holmes. 'This last drawing is very important. It makes me feel hopeful. Please continue your interesting story.'

'I've nothing more to say,' replied Hilton Cubitt, 'except, I was angry with Elsie for holding me back. I'm sure she knows who this man is and what these pictures mean.

'Now I must go back to Norfolk. Elsie is very frightened and I don't want to leave her alone at night.'

'Well,' said Holmes, 'please leave these pictures with me. I will examine them carefully. I think I'll be able to solve the mystery soon.'

4

Terrible News

As soon as Hilton Cubitt left the room, Holmes ran to a table. He put all the papers with pictures of dancing men on the table. He began to examine them carefully.

For the next two hours, Holmes worked hard examining the papers. At last, he jumped up excitedly. Then he sat down again and wrote out a long telegram[22].

31

'As soon as we get an answer to this telegram, Watson,' he said, 'we'll visit Mr Cubitt in Norfolk. I have some important information for him.'

I was very curious about the telegram. I very much wanted to know what Holmes had found out about the meaning of the dancing men. But I didn't ask any questions. I knew Holmes would tell me when he was ready.

Two days passed. Then on the evening of the second day, Holmes received another letter from Hilton Cubitt.

In this letter, Mr Cubitt said he had found a new drawing of dancing men. He had found the drawing that morning, on the sundial in the garden. Mr Cubitt had made a copy of the drawing in his letter:

Holmes examined these pictures carefully. Suddenly he jumped up.

'We must go to Norfolk at once, Watson,' he said.

At that moment, a telegram arrived for Holmes. It was the answer he had been waiting for. Holmes read the telegram and his face looked serious.

'Mr Cubitt is in terrible danger,' he said. 'He needs our help.'

But, unfortunately, we were not able to go to Norfolk that evening. It was late and the last train had gone. The next train was not until the morning. In the morning, we travelled to Norfolk. At the station, we asked our way to Ridling Thorpe Manor.

'Are you the detectives from London?' the stationmaster asked.

'Why do you think we are detectives from London?' asked Holmes in surprise.

'Because the Norfolk police are already on their way to

Ridling Thorpe Manor,' said the stationmaster. 'But perhaps you are doctors? The lady isn't dead yet. You may be in time to save her life.'

Holmes looked very worried.

'What do you mean?' he asked. 'What has happened at Ridling Thorpe Manor?'

'It's terrible news,' replied the stationmaster. 'Both Mr Hilton Cubitt and his wife have been shot. Mr Cubitt is dead and his wife is seriously injured.'

5

The Investigation Begins

At once, Holmes hurried to a carriage. During the journey to Ridling Thorpe Manor, he did not speak at all. But I could see he was very worried.

Holmes had known that Hilton Cubitt was in danger. But he had not arrived in time to save his client.

At last, we could see a large, old house through the trees. This was Ridling Thorpe Manor. As we came near the front door, I saw the toolhouse and the sundial in the garden. These were the places where Hilton Cubitt had found pictures of dancing men.

A carriage was standing outside the front door and a small man was getting out. This man introduced himself as Inspector Martin of the Norfolk police. Holmes introduced himself to Inspector Martin.

Inspector Martin was very surprised when he heard my friend's name.

'But, Mr Holmes,' he said, 'the crime was committed[23] only a few hours ago, at three o'clock this morning! How did you get here from London so quickly?'

'When I left London, I didn't know a crime had been committed,' replied Holmes. 'I was on my way here to prevent a crime. But I've arrived too late.

'Now, Inspector Martin, shall we work together on this investigation[24]? Or do you want to work alone?'

'I'd be very pleased to work with you,' replied the inspector.

'Good,' said Holmes. 'Then let's try to find out what happened.'

At that moment, the doctor, an old, white-haired man, came downstairs from Mrs Cubitt's room. The doctor said the lady was very badly injured, but that she would not die.

The bullet which wounded Mrs Cubitt had gone into her brain. The gun which fired the bullet had been very close to her. Hilton Cubitt had been shot through the heart.

A gun had been found lying halfway between the two bodies. Two shots had been fired from the gun.

But we did not know if Mrs Cubitt had shot her husband first, and then shot herself. Or if Mr Cubitt had shot his wife, and then killed himself.

'Has Mr Cubitt's body been moved?' asked Holmes.

'No,' replied the doctor. 'We had to move the lady. We couldn't leave her lying injured on the floor.'

'Who found the body?'

'Two of the servants,' said the doctor.

'Then let's hear their story,' said Holmes.

The two women told their story very clearly. They had been awakened from their sleep by a loud noise. A minute later, they heard another noise.

Both women ran downstairs from their rooms. The door of a downstairs room was open and Mr Cubitt lay dead on the floor.

Near the window, his wife was sitting with her head against the wall. One side of her face was red with blood.

The window was shut and the room was full of smoke and the smell of gunpowder.

Mr Cubitt lay dead on the floor. His wife was sitting with her
head against the wall.

Immediately, the two servants sent for the doctor. When he arrived, they carried Mrs Cubitt upstairs.

The servants did not understand why the crime had been committed. Mr and Mrs Cubitt had been in love with each other and had never quarrelled.

'Tell me,' said Holmes, 'when did you first notice the smell of gunpowder?'

'When we ran out of our rooms upstairs,' replied the women.

'Good,' said Holmes. 'Now let's examine the room downstairs.'

6

Holmes Sends a Note

The room was small, with a window looking onto the garden. Mr Cubitt's body lay on the floor.

'You can take away the body now,' said Holmes. Then he turned to the doctor. 'Have you found the bullet which injured Mrs Cubitt?' he asked.

'No,' replied the doctor. 'The bullet is still somewhere in her brain. We will have to operate to remove the bullet.'

'We know that two bullets were fired from the gun,' said Inspector Martin. 'And we know where each bullet went. One bullet killed Mr Cubitt and the other injured his wife.'

'Yes,' said Holmes, 'but what about the third bullet – the bullet which passed through the window frame[25]?'

He turned suddenly and pointed to a hole in the bottom of the window frame. This hole was the exact shape and size of a bullet.

'Wonderful!' cried Inspector Martin. 'Then three shots were fired, not two. A third person was in the room.

'But, Mr Holmes, how did you know a bullet had passed through the window frame?'

'Well,' said Holmes, 'you remember that the two servants smelt gunpowder as soon as they left their rooms?'

'Yes,' said the Inspector, 'but I still don't understand.'

'The servants' rooms are upstairs. But the gun was fired *downstairs*. So the smell of the gunpowder must have been blown from this room to the rooms upstairs. Therefore the window must have been open.

'A third person could have stood outside the window and fired through it. If somebody inside the room fired at this person and missed, the bullet would pass through the window frame.'

'I understand,' said Inspector Martin. 'But when the servants entered this room, they said the window was shut.'

'That was because Mrs Cubitt had just shut it,' replied Holmes. 'But what's this?'

A lady's handbag was standing on a small table. I saw it was full of money. The money was tied together. We counted twenty fifty-pound notes.

'This money is important evidence[26],' said Holmes. 'And now let's find out where the third bullet went, after it passed through the window frame.'

We all went outside into the garden. There were flowers planted underneath the window. The flowers were broken and there were large footprints on the ground.

Holmes searched in the grass. Suddenly he bent forward and picked something up. It was the missing bullet.

'I think, Inspector,' he said, 'that our case is nearly solved.'

'But, Mr Holmes,' said the Inspector, 'who was this other person and how did he get away?'

'I will tell you later,' said Holmes. 'First, I want to know if there is a place near here called Elrige's?'

We asked the servants, but none of them had ever heard the name. Then the boy who worked with the horses remembered a farm with that name. This farm was a very lonely place, many miles away, near a village called East Rushton.

Holmes thought for a moment, then he smiled strangely.

'Bring a horse,' he said to the boy. 'I want you to take a message to Elrige's Farm.'

Then Holmes took from his pocket all the papers with the pictures of the dancing men on them. He sat down at a table and worked carefully. Finally, he handed a note to the boy.

'Give this note to the person whose name is written on the outside,' said Holmes. 'And don't answer any questions.'

I looked at the outside of the note. It was addressed, in large writing, to:

> *Mr Abe Slaney,*
> *Elrige's Farm,*
> *East Rushton,*
> *Norfolk*

Then Holmes turned to Inspector Martin.

'I think you should get more policemen,' he said. 'We'll have to catch a dangerous criminal.'

7

Holmes Explains the Mystery

After the boy had left, Holmes gave some instructions to the servants.

'If anybody comes and asks for Mrs Cubitt,' he said, 'do not tell the person that she is ill. Show the person straight into the sitting-room.

'There are some things I want to explain,' Holmes said. Then he told the Inspector about Hilton Cubitt's visits to us in London and the pictures of the dancing men.

'These drawings are a kind of secret writing,' said Holmes. 'They look like children's drawings, but they are messages. Each picture of a dancing man is a letter of the alphabet. Let me show you how it works.

'The letter of the alphabet which appears most often in English is "E". The picture of the dancing man which appeared most often was 🕺 So I knew that this picture was "E".

'Some of the dancing men were holding flags. I guessed that a figure with a flag was the last letter of a word.'

'But how did you find out what the other pictures meant?' I asked.

'On Hilton Cubitt's second visit,' went on Holmes, 'he brought three different messages with him. The last message was:

'In this message, there was no flag. So the message had to be one, single word. What could it be?

'The word had five letters, and the second and fourth letters were "E". It might be "Sever" or "LEVER" or "NEVER". But the most probable of these words was "NEVER". So I knew the

pictures 🕺, 🕺 and 🕺 were "N", "V" and "R".'

'Excellent, Holmes!' I cried. 'What did you do next?'

'Well,' said Holmes, 'I knew Mrs Cubitt's first name was Elsie. I noticed that there was another word which had five letters and began and ended with "E".

'So I guessed that ⚘ , ⚘ and ⚘ probably were "L", "S" and "I".

'In one message, the word "ELSIE" was written twice. In this message, the word before "ELSIE" had four letters and ended with "E". I guessed the writer was asking Elsie to do something.

'So now I looked for an English word of four letters ending in "E". The best word I could think of was "COME".

'So now I knew that ⚘ , ⚘ and ⚘ were "C", "O" and "M".

'Then I looked again at the first message which Hilton Cubitt brought us:

'I used the figures holding flags to divide the message into words. I wrote out the message, putting dots for the letters I didn't know.

.M .ERE ..E SL.NE.

'The first missing letter had to be "A" and the second letter had to be "H".

AM HERE A.E SLANE.

'Clearly, the two missing letters were part of somebody's name. So it must be:

AM HERE ABE SLANEY

'Then I looked at the second message again:

'This message worked out like this:

A. ELRI.ES

'Here, I worked out that the missing letters could be "T" and "G".

AT ELRIGES

'I decided to find out if there was a place near Ridling Thorpe Manor that was called Elrige's. If there was, then I knew that this was where the writer of the messages was staying.'

Inspector Martin and I looked at Holmes. It was wonderful how my friend had found out the meaning of the dancing men.

'What did you do then, Mr Holmes?' asked the Inspector.

'I guessed that Abe Slaney was an American. "Abe" is an American name and Mrs Cubitt had recently received a letter from America. This letter had upset her very much.

'So I sent a telegram to a friend in the New York Police, asking about Abe Slaney. This was the reply:

THE MOST DANGEROUS CROOK[27] IN CHICAGO

'The same evening, I received Hilton Cubitt's final message.

The message worked out like this:

ELSIE . RE.ARE TO MEET THY GO.

Clearly, the missing letters had to be "P" and "D".

ELSIE PREPARE TO MEET THY GOD

'I knew the Cubitts were in terrible danger. Abe Slaney was saying he was going to kill Mrs Cubitt. So Dr Watson and I hurried immediately to Norfolk, but, unfortunately, we were too late. Hilton Cubitt was dead.'

'But what about Abe Slaney, Mr Holmes?' asked Inspector Martin. If he is the murderer and he's at Elrige's, he may escape.

'Don't worry,' said Holmes. 'He won't escape. He's coming here.'

'Here?' said Inspector Martin, in surprise. 'Why should he come here?'

'Because I have written and asked him to come here.'

Holmes stood up and walked to the window. 'Look, here he is!'

8

The Murderer is Caught

A man was coming up the path. He was tall and handsome, with a large, black beard. The front doorbell rang loudly.

'Hide behind the door,' said Holmes quietly. 'This man is very dangerous and we must be careful.'

We waited in silence for a minute. Then the sitting-room door opened and the man stepped into the room. At once, Holmes put a gun against his head and Inspector Martin put handcuffs[25] on his wrists.

The man looked at us. His black eyes looked angry.

'I received a note from Mrs Cubitt,' he said. 'Where is she?'

'Mrs Cubitt is badly injured,' replied Holmes. 'Her life is in great danger.'

The man cried out. He sat down on a chair and put his face in his hands.

'I didn't know she was injured,' he said. 'I shot her husband when he tried to kill me. But I would never injure Elsie. I love her more than anything in the world.'

Suddenly the man looked up.

'Wait,' he said. 'If Elsie is badly injured, who wrote this?'

He opened his hands and threw a note onto the table.

'I wrote it, to make you come here,' said Holmes.

'You wrote it? But how could you know the meaning of the dancing men?'

'I worked out what the figures meant,' replied Holmes. 'But now, tell us your story.'

'All right,' said the man. 'If Elsie dies, it doesn't matter what happens to me.

'My name is Abe Slaney and I've known Elsie since she was a child. Her father was head of a gang of crooks in Chicago and I was a member of the gang.

'Elsie's father thought of the secret writing of the dancing men. The members of the gang used it to send messages to one another.

'Elsie and I were engaged to be married. But Elsie hated her father's business and she didn't want to be married to a criminal. So she ran away to England. She met and married this Englishman, Hilton Cubitt.

'I wrote to Elsie, but she didn't answer my letters. In the end, I came to England and stayed at Elrige's Farm.

'I knew Elsie understood the pictures of the dancing men. So I

At once, Holmes put a gun against his head and Inspector Martin put handcuffs on his wrists.

left messages where she would see them. In the messages, I asked her to come away with me. But her only answer was "Never".

'Then Elsie wrote me a letter. She said she would meet me at three o'clock in the morning, when her husband was asleep.

'She brought money with her. She offered me the money and asked me to go away. I became angry and tried to pull her through the window.

'Just then, her husband rushed in, carrying a gun. He fired the gun at me and missed. At the same moment, I shot at him and he fell down dead.

'I ran across the garden. As I ran, I heard the window shut behind me.

'I have told you the truth, gentlemen. I didn't know Elsie was hurt. She must have shot herself after I left.'

While Abe Slaney was talking, a carriage arrived with two policemen in it. Inspector Martin turned to his prisoner.

'It's time for us to go, Slaney. Goodbye, Mr Holmes. I hope I'll work with you again one day.'

As the carriage drove away, I saw the note which Abe Slaney had thrown on the table. This was what Holmes had written:

'If you work it out, Watson,' said Holmes, 'you'll find it means: "Come here at once".

'I knew Abe Slaney would come when he read the note. He would think Mrs Cubitt had written it.'

'Well,' I said, 'criminals have used the dancing men to help them in their crimes. But now the dancing men have been used to catch a criminal.'

'Yes,' said Holmes. 'The dancing men have finally done some good.'

45

THE RED-HEADED LEAGUE

1

A Strange Advertisement

After my marriage, I lived with my wife in another part of London. My friend, Sherlock Holmes, continued to live in his apartment in Baker Street.

One day, in the autumn of 1890, I decided to visit my friend. But when I arrived at his apartment, I found he already had a visitor.

This visitor was an old man. He was fat, with a red face. But the most unusual thing about him was his hair. The colour of the old man's hair was bright red.

'I'm sorry, Holmes,' I said. 'I didn't know you were busy. I'll wait in the next room.'

But Holmes didn't want me to leave. He pulled me into the room and closed the door.

'This is my friend, Dr Watson,' he said to the old man. 'Dr Watson has helped me with many cases. Perhaps he can also help me with yours.'

'I'm very interested in your cases, Holmes,' I said.

'This is Mr Jabez Wilson,' went on Holmes. The old man nodded to me. 'Mr Wilson has come to me with a very unusual story. It's the most interesting problem I've heard for a long time.

'Mr Wilson, could you please tell your story again from the beginning. I'd like Dr Watson to hear it.'

Mr Wilson pulled an old newspaper out of his pocket. He opened the paper on his knees and turned to the advertisement[29] page. He ran his finger down the advertisements and pointed to one of them.

'Here,' he said. 'This is how everything began. Read it for yourself, Dr Watson.'

I took the newspaper from Mr Wilson. It was *The Morning Chronicle* and was two months old. I read the advertisement:

THE-RED HEADED LEAGUE[30]:
Another vacancy[31] is open for someone wishing to
become a member of the League. Salary – four pounds
a week. All red-headed men, over 21 years old,
should come on Monday at 11 a.m. to this address:
Duncan Ross, The Red-Headed League,
7 Pope's Court, Fleet Street, London.

2

The Red-Headed League

'What a strange advertisement,' I said. 'Whatever can it mean?'

Holmes laughed.

'It's very unusual, isn't it,' he said. 'And now, Mr Wilson, tell us your story.'

'Well,' began Mr Wilson, 'I have a small shop in Saxe-Coburg Square, in the City of London.

'But business hasn't been good for some time and I don't make much money any more. I used to have two assistants, but now I can only pay one. My assistant is very interested in learning the business. So he's willing to work for half-pay.'

'That's very unusual,' said Holmes. 'What's the name of your assistant?'

'Vincent Spaulding,' replied Mr Wilson. 'He's an excellent assistant, but he does do one unusual thing.

'Spaulding's very interested in photography and takes a lot of photographs. He develops[32] these photographs himself, in the cellar of my shop. When he isn't working, he spends all his time down there.'

'Go on,' said Holmes.

'We live very quietly,' continued Mr Wilson. 'I don't go out very much. And I don't read the newspapers.

'One day, eight weeks ago, Spaulding came to me with a newspaper in his hand. It was the same newspaper that I showed you, Dr Watson.

' "Mr Wilson," said Spaulding, "I wish I were a red headed man."

' "Why?" I asked in surprise.

' "Well, here's another vacancy in The Red-Headed League," replied Spaulding.

' "The Red-headed League?" I asked. "What's that?"

'Spaulding looked at me and laughed.

' "Haven't you ever heard of The Red-Headed League?" he said. "You could become a member and make a lot of money."

'Well, when I heard that,' said Mr Wilson, 'at once I became very interested. I needed more money. So I asked Spaulding to tell me more about this Red-Headed League.

' "I think," said Spaulding, "the League was started by an American called Ezekiah Hopkins. Ezekiah Hopkins was a very rich man and enjoyed doing unusual things.

' "Hopkins was red-headed himself and liked all other red-headed men. So when he died, he left his money in his will to help red-headed men. The money was used to start The Red-Headed League. When a man became a member, he would be paid an excellent salary for very little work.

' "And now," said Spaulding, showing me the advertisement again, here's another vacancy in the League. Why don't you go to Pope's Court, Mr Wilson? I'm sure you could become a member!"

'Now as you see, gentlemen,' continued Mr Wilson, 'the colour of my hair is bright red. So I thought I could easily become a member of this Red-Headed League.

'Vincent Spaulding seemed to know a lot about the League. So I asked him to come with me to the address in the advertisement.

'We closed the shop for the day and set off for Pope's Court, Fleet Street.'

3

An Unusual Job

Holmes rubbed his hands together and smiled. 'Your story is very interesting, Mr Wilson,' he said. 'Please go on.'

'When we arrived in Fleet Street,' said Mr Wilson, 'we saw a strange thing. The whole street was full of red-headed men. They had all come to answer the advertisement.

'When I saw how many men were waiting, I wanted to go home. But Spaulding wouldn't let me. He pushed and pulled me through the crowd. At last, we reached the stairs leading up to the office in Pope's Court.

'A small man was sitting behind a table. The colour of this man's hair was a brighter red than my own.

' "This is Mr Jabez Wilson," said my assistant. "He has come about the vacancy in the League."

'He pushed and pulled me through the crowd.'

'The small man looked carefully at my hair. He looked at it for such a long time, that I began to feel uncomfortable. Suddenly he bent forward and grabbed my hair with both hands. He pulled at it until I cried out in pain.

' "I'm sorry I hurt you," said the man. Your hair is a wonderful colour. But I had to make sure you weren't wearing a wig. I had to find out if your hair was real."

'Then he went over to the window. He opened it and shouted down to the men below that the vacancy was taken. The red-headed men groaned with disappointment. Then they began to walk away. In a few minutes, the square was empty.

' "My name," said the small man, is Duncan Ross. You are now a member of The Red-Headed League. When can you start the job?"

' "Well, that's going to be difficult," I replied. "I have a business already."

' "Oh, don't worry about that, Mr Wilson!" cried Spaulding. "I can look after the business for you."

'Now I knew that my assistant was a good worker and would look after my business well. So I asked Duncan Ross, "What are the hours of work?"

' "Every day, between the hours of ten o'clock and two o'clock," replied Mr Ross. "The pay is four pounds a week. But you must not leave the office at any time between ten and two. If you leave for any reason, you'll lose your pay."

' "I understand," I said. "And what is the work?"

' "Copying out the *Encyclopaedia Britannica*[33]. The first book of it is over there. Will you be able to start work tomorrow?"

' "Certainly," I said.

' "Then goodbye, Mr Wilson. I hope you enjoy your work."

'I went home with Vincent Spaulding. I was very pleased. It was an easy job to copy out the *Encyclopaedia Britannica* and the pay was excellent.

'Next morning, when I arrived at the office, Duncan Ross was waiting for me. I started copying out the *Encyclopaedia*, beginning with subjects under the letter 'A'. Sometimes Mr Ross left the room, but he kept coming back to see me.

'At two o'clock, he told me I had worked well. He was very pleased. Then I left and he locked the office door behind me.

'The same thing happened every day for eight weeks. Every morning, I began work at ten, and every afternoon, I left at two. Every Saturday, I was given four pounds for my week's work.

'At first, Mr Ross came into the office to watch me work. But after a time, he stopped coming. However, I was afraid to leave the office. I didn't want to lose my pay.

'But suddenly everything came to an end.'

'To an end?' asked Holmes.

'Yes. This morning, I went to work as usual at ten o'clock. But the door was locked and on it was this card.'

Mr Wilson held up a small piece of white card. This is what it said:

THE RED-HEADED LEAGUE IS FINISHED
9th October 1890

4

Who is Vincent Spaulding?

Holmes and I looked at the piece of white card. Then we looked at Mr Wilson's face. He looked very disappointed and upset. But there was also something rather funny about The Red-Headed League. Suddenly we both began to laugh.

'I don't think this is funny!' cried Mr Wilson angrily. 'Perhaps I should take my case somewhere else.'

'No, no,' said Holmes. 'Your case is most interesting and unusual. What did you do when you found the card on the door?'

'I was extremely surprised,' replied Mr Wilson. 'I didn't know what to do. I went to all the offices in the building. I asked if anyone knew anything about The Red-Headed League. But no one had ever heard of Duncan Ross.

'At last, I went home to Saxe-Coburg Square. I told Vincent Spaulding what had happened. Spaulding said that if I waited, perhaps the League would write to me. Perhaps they would explain everything in a letter.

'But I didn't want to wait. I've lost a good salary of four pounds a week. I want to find out about this League and why they did this to me.

'Mr Holmes, I've heard you help people when they are in trouble. That's why I've come to you.'

'You've done the right thing,' said Holmes. 'I'll be happy to help you, Mr Wilson. But first, I want to ask you some questions.

'Your assistant – Vincent Spaulding – how long had he been with you before he saw the advertisement?'

'About a month.'

'How did he get the job as your assistant?'

'I advertised the vacancy for an assistant. He came for the job. I chose him because he looked a good worker. Also, he said that he would work for half-pay.'

'What does Spaulding look like?'

'He's small and he moves very quickly. He's about thirty years old and has a white mark on his forehead.'

Holmes sat up straight in his chair. He was very excited. 'Tell me,' he said, 'is there anything unusual about Vincent Spaulding's ears?'

'Yes,' replied Mr Wilson. 'They have holes in them for

earrings. He told me a gypsy did this when he was a boy.'

Holmes sat back in his chair. He was thinking carefully. I guessed Holmes already knew something about Vincent Spaulding.

'Is Spaulding still working for you?' asked Holmes.

'Yes,' said Mr Wilson. 'I've left him at the shop.'

'Good. Mr Wilson, I need a couple of days to investigate this case. I hope to solve the mystery by Monday.'

After Mr Wilson had left Holmes turned to me.

'Well, Watson,' he said, 'what do you think about all this?'

'I can't understand it,' I said. 'It's most unusual.'

'I need to think,' said Holmes. 'Please don't speak to me for at least fifty minutes. I'm going to smoke my pipe.'

Holmes sat back in his chair. He put his black pipe between his lips, lit it and closed his eyes. Time passed. I thought Holmes had fallen asleep.

But suddenly Holmes jumped out of his chair and put his pipe down on the table.

'Watson,' he said, 'we're going to visit Saxe-Coburg Square. Come quickly!'

5

A Visit to Saxe-Coburg Square

We soon arrived in Saxe-Coburg Square, the place where Mr Wilson had his shop.

Saxe-Coburg Square was in a poor part of London. It was a small and quiet square. On each side of the square stood a line of old houses. In the middle of the square was a small garden with grass.

Sherlock Holmes stopped outside one of the houses on the corner of the square. On the wall of this house, there was a brown notice, with the words 'Jabez Wilson', in white letters.

Holmes walked up and down and examined all the houses, carefully. Then, he returned to Mr Wilson's house. Suddenly, he hit the pavement outside the house with his stick.

Then he went up to the house and knocked on the door. Immediately, it was opened by a young man. This was Mr Wilson's assistant, Vincent Spaulding.

'Excuse me,' said Holmes, 'can you please tell me the way to the Strand?'

'Go down the third street on the right,' answered the assistant quickly. Then he closed the door.

'That's a very clever young man,' said Holmes, as we walked away. 'I know something about him. I believe he's the fourth cleverest man in London.'

'It is clear,' I said, 'that Mr Wilson's assistant plays an important part in the mystery of The Red-Headed League. Did you ask the way to the Strand in order to get a look at him?'

'No,' said Holmes, 'but I wanted to look at the knees of his trousers.'

'The knees of his trousers!' I cried in astonishment. 'Well then, Holmes, why did you hit the pavement?'

'Watson,' said Holmes, 'we haven't time to talk now. We've seen the front of Saxe-Coburg Square. Let's now investigate the street at the back.'

We went round the corner and walked to the street at the back of Mr Wilson's shop. We were immediately in one of the busiest and most important streets in the City of London.

A line of expensive shops and important businesses were on the side of the road. Hundreds of people were hurrying along the pavements and the roadway was busy with traffic.

It was hard to believe that Saxe-Coburg Square, with its poor,

*Holmes knocked on the door. Immediately, it was opened
by a young man.*

old houses, was immediately behind the important buildings of this busy street.

Holmes looked along the line of buildings.

'This is very interesting, Watson,' said Holmes. 'There's a tobacconist's, a newspaper shop, a restaurant and – ah yes, the offices of the City and Suburban Bank!'

I could see that Holmes was very excited.

'Well, Watson, I have some work to do that will take a few hours,' went on Holmes. 'This case at Saxe-Coburg Square is serious.'

'Serious!' I said. 'Why?'

'An important crime has been planned. I think we'll be in time to stop it. But I'll need your help tonight.'

'At what time?'

'Ten o'clock.'

'Then I'll be at your apartment at ten.'

'Good. And, Watson – there may be some danger, so please bring your gun with you.'

I said goodbye and went home. I thought about everything that had happened. It was a very strange case and I did not understand what was happening. Where were we going that evening? What were we going to do? Why did I have to bring my gun? And who was Vincent Spaulding?

There was only one thing to do. I had to wait until the evening. Then perhaps I would get the answers to these questions.

6

Everything is Ready

At quarter past nine that evening, I set off for Baker Street, where Holmes lived. When I arrived, I noticed two carriages standing outside Holmes' door.

Inside his apartment, Holmes was talking with two men. One of them was Peter Jones, a police detective. The other man was tall and thin, with a sad-looking face.

'Hello, Watson,' said Holmes. 'I think you already know Mr Jones, of Scotland Yard? Let me introduce Mr Merryweather. Mr Merryweather is also coming with us tonight.'

'I hope it's important,' said Mr Merryweather sadly. 'I usually play cards with friends on Saturday evenings. I have played cards every Saturday night for the last twenty-seven years.'

'I think,' said Sherlock Holmes, 'that tonight you'll play a more exciting game than cards. You, Mr Merryweather, may lose thirty thousand pounds. You, Jones, may win the prize of a criminal you want to catch.'

'The criminal John Clay, murderer and thief,' said Jones. 'He's a young man, but he's a very clever criminal. I want to catch him more than any criminal in London.'

'It's time to go now,' said Holmes. 'Two carriages are waiting. You two take the first carriage and Watson and I will follow in the second.'

The carriages went quickly through the dark streets. I wondered where we were going.

'We're nearly there,' Holmes said to me, at last. 'This man, Merryweather, is a bank manager. I wanted Jones to come with us, too. He's a good man. He's not very clever, but he is very brave. Ah, here we are.'

We were in the same busy street which Holmes and I had

visited earlier in the day. We got out of the carriages and Mr Merryweather took us down to a small side door. Through the door was a corridor with an iron gate at the end.

Mr Merryweather opened this gate and stopped to light a lantern. Then he took us down some steps and through another gate. At last, we were in a large cellar. This cellar was full of large boxes.

Holmes took out his magnifying glass[34] and went down on his knees to the floor. He examined the stones on the floor, then he jumped up and put the glass back in his pocket.

'We have about an hour,' he said. 'The criminals will wait until Mr Wilson is in bed. Then they'll move quickly.

'Watson, we're in the cellar of one of the most important banks in London. Mr Merryweather is the manager of this bank. He'll explain why the criminals are interested in this cellar at the moment.'

'About two months ago,' whispered Mr Merryweather, 'the bank received a huge amount of gold from the Bank of France. But we never used the money. It's still Lying in boxes in this cellar.'

'I understand,' I said.

'Well,' said Holmes, 'let's make our plans. Mr Merryweather, you must put out the lantern. But first we must decide where to stand. These men are dangerous and we must move carefully.

'I want you all to hide behind these boxes. When I shine my light on the men, attack them. If they fire a gun, Watson, shoot back at once.'

I hid behind a wooden box and put my gun on the top. Merryweather put out the lantern and we were in complete darkness. 'They have only one way of escape,' whispered Holmes. 'That's back through Wilson's shop, into Saxe-Coburg Square. Have you done what I asked you, Jones?'

'Three police officers are waiting at the front door of Wilson's shop,' replied Jones.

'Excellent! Then everything is ready. And now, we must be silent and wait.'

Holmes took out his magnifying glass and went down on his knees to the floor.

7

The Capture of John Clay

More than an hour went by. My arms and legs were tired, but I was afraid to move. The only sound was the breathing of my three companions.

Suddenly I saw a light. This light was coming from underneath the floor. It was shining between the stones in the floor. Slowly, one of the large stones turned over on its side. There was now a large, square hole in the floor. The light of a lantern shone up through this hole.

I saw a face appear in the hole. By the light of the lantern, I recognised Mr Wilson's assistant.

The young man pulled himself up out of the hole. He turned round and stood beside the hole. Then he began to pull up another man after him. This man was thin and small, with bright red hair.

'Let's hurry,' whispered the young man.

Suddenly Holmes jumped forward and grabbed the young man by the neck. Immediately, the man with red hair jumped down the hole again. Jones grabbed at his coat and I heard the sound of tearing cloth.

At once the young man pulled a gun out of his pocket. But Holmes hit the man's hand and the gun fell to the floor.

'Stand still, John Clay,' said Holmes. 'You cannot escape.'

'All right,' replied the young man. 'But I think my friend has escaped.'

'You'll see your friend very soon,' said Jones. 'There are three policemen waiting for him at the front door.

'Now then, John Clay, please hold out your hands. I'm going to take you to the police station.'

Jones put the handcuffs on John Clay's wrists, then led him

But Holmes hit the man's hand and the gun fell to the floor.

upstairs. Holmes, Mr Merryweather and I followed them from the cellar.

'Mr Holmes,' said Mr Merryweather, 'I don't know how the bank can thank you. You've stopped a very serious crime.'

'Well,' replied Holmes, 'I've wanted to catch John Clay for a long time. And this has been a very interesting case. I enjoyed hearing the strange story of The Red-Headed League.'

8

The Mystery Explained

Later, Holmes explained to me the mystery of The Red-Headed League.

'You see, Watson,' he said, 'it was clear that the men in The Red-Headed League wanted only one thing. They wanted to get Mr Wilson out of his shop for some hours every day. That was why they kept him busy, copying out the *Encyclopaedia Britannica*.

'John Clay is a very clever young man. It was he who thought of The Red-Headed League. He thought of it because Mr Wilson's hair was the same colour as his friend's hair – very bright red.

'Clay put the advertisement in the newspaper. Then he showed the advertisement to Mr Wilson. He suggested to Mr Wilson that he should apply for the vacancy in the League.

'When Mr Wilson told us that his assistant was working for half-pay, I knew he must have a special reason for wanting the job.'

'But Holmes,' I said, 'how could you know what that reason was?'

'Mr Wilson's business is small,' explained Holmes. 'There was nothing *inside* his house to attract criminals. So I knew it must be something *outside* the house. What could it be?

'Mr Wilson told us that Vincent Spaulding – or John Clay – spent many hours in the cellar. The cellar! He was doing something in the cellar.

'I asked more questions about Vincent Spaulding. I found out that he was John Clay, one of London's most dangerous criminals. What could John Clay want in Wilson's cellar? I could think of only one answer. He must be digging a tunnel to another building.

'Then we visited Saxe-Coburg Square and I surprised you by knocking on the pavement with my stick. I wanted to find out exactly where the cellar was. I knew, from the sound my stick made, that there was no cellar in front of the house. Then I rang the doorbell and Clay answered it. I saw that the knees of his trousers were dirty. Clearly, he had been digging for many hours.

'But what was he digging for? I walked round the corner, saw the City and Suburban Bank and knew that I had solved the problem. When you went home, I visited Jones and Mr Merryweather and asked them to come with us tonight.'

'How did you know the animals would try to rob the bank tonight?' I asked.

'When they closed The Red-Headed League office,' said Holmes, 'I knew the tunnel was finished. The criminals were ready to move.

'Today is Saturday. No one would come to the bank until Monday. If they took the gold tonight, they would have two days for their escape.'

'Excellent, Holmes!' I said. 'You have been very clever. You have solved another difficult case.'

POINTS
FOR
UNDERSTANDING

Points for Understanding

THE SPECKLED BAND

1

1 Who is:
   (a) Sherlock Holmes?
   (b) Dr Watson?
2 Why did Sherlock Holmes wake up Dr Watson?
3 Why was the lady shivering?
4 What was unusual about the lady's hair?

2

1 What was Helen Stoner's sister's first name?
2 When the two young girls were only two years old, what did their mother do?
3 Where did Dr Roylott live?
4 When Mrs Roylott died, what would happen to her money?
5 What happened to Mrs Roylott?
6 Who were Dr Roylott's only friends?
7 What kind of animals did Dr Roylott have?
8 What happened two weeks before Julia's wedding?

3

1 Describe the position of the three bedrooms at Stoke Moran.
2 One night, Julia asked Helen a strange question.
   (a) What was the question?
   (b) What did Helen suggest might be the answer to Julia's question?
3 Why did Julia and Helen always lock their doors at night?
4 When Helen Stoner heard her sister scream, she ran into the corridor. What two strange noises did she hear?
5 What words did Julia cry out before she fainted?
6 How did Holmes know that Julia had lit a match to see round her?
7 Why was it certain that Julia was alone in her bedroom?
8 What was, Helen Stoner's explanation of Julia's strange words?

9   Two strange things had happened at Stoke Moran.
        (a) Why did Helen have to move out of her bedroom?
        (b) Which bedroom did she move into?
        (c) What strange noise did she hear last night?

4

1   What marks did Holmes notice on Helen Stoner's arm?
2   Why did Holmes want to visit Stoke Moran?
3   What did Dr Roylott tell Holmes to do?
4   Why did Dr Roylott bend the poker?
5   How did Holmes show that he was as strong as Dr Roylott?

5

1   How did Holmes and Watson get to Dr Roylott's house?
    Who was the first person they saw when they arrived?
2   What did Holmes think was very unusual about:
        (a) the work being done to Helen's bedroom?
        (b) the bell-rope in Julia's bedroom?
        (c) the ventilator?
3   Why did Holmes ask if there was a cat in the safe?
4   What was strange about the stick lying on the bed?
5   Where did Holmes want to wait that night?

6

1   What did Holmes ask Helen Stoner to do when she heard Dr
    Roylott go to bed?
2   What would Holmes and Watson do when they saw the lamp in the
    bedroom window?
3   Holmes told Watson that they might be in great danger that night.
        (a) What was unusual about the bell-rope?
        (b) What was unusual about the ventilator?
        (c) What was unusual about the bed?

7

1 What frightened Dr Watson in the garden at Stoke Moran?
2 Why would Dr Watson never forget that night?
3 What strange noise did Watson hear?
4 What did Holmes do when he heard the noise?
5 What was the 'speckled band'?

8

1 How did the snake come from the next door bedroom?
2 How did Dr Roylott make the snake come back to him?
3 What was the loud, clanging noise which Helen had heard?
4 Why was Holmes not sorry for Dr Roylott?

THE DANCING MEN

1

1 Why had Hilton Cubitt come to see Sherlock Holmes?
2 Mr Cubitt showed Holmes some strange drawings. What did they look like?

2

1 How long has Mr Cubitt's family lived at Ridling Thorpe Manor?
2 Mr Cubitt made a promise to his wife before they got married.
   (a) What was the promise?
   (b) Had Mr Cubitt kept his promise?
3 What happened when Mrs Cubitt received a letter from America?
4 Why would Mrs Cubitt never do anything to upset her husband?
5 Mr Cubitt found a piece of paper on the sundial in the garden.
   (a) What was on the paper?
   (b) What happened when he showed the paper to his wife?
6 Why did Mr Cubitt not want to go to the police?
7 What did Holmes ask Mr Cubitt to do?

3

1 About a fortnight later, Mr Cubitt came back to see Sherlock Holmes.
    (a) What did he bring with him?
    (b) What else had he seen?
2 Mr Cubitt had his gun in his hand and started to run out of the house.
    (a) What did he want to do?
    (b) What did his wife do?
3 Hilton Cubitt was sure that his wife knew more about the mystery than she had told him. What else did he think she knew?
4 How did Sherlock Holmes think he could solve the mystery?

4

1 What did Holmes do after studying the pictures of the dancing men?
2 What made Holmes sure that Hilton Cubitt was in great danger?
3 Why were Holmes and Watson not able to go to Ridling Thorpe Manor that evening?
4 What terrible news did the stationmaster give Holmes and Watson?

5

1 Why was Inspector Martin surprised at the arrival of Holmes and Watson?
2 What had happened to:
    (a) Hilton Cubitt?
    (b) Mrs Cubitt?
3 How many shots had been fired from the gun lying between the two bodies?
4 When did the servants first notice the smell of gunpowder?

6

1 Why was Holmes sure that:
    (a) more than two shots had been fired?
    (b) the window had been open?
2 Where could a third person have stood?
3 Who did Holmes say had shut the window?
4 What did they find in the lady's handbag?
5 What did Holmes find in the grass outside the window?
6 Holmes sat down and wrote a note. Who was this note addressed to?

7

1 Holmes explained the meaning of the drawings.
    (a) What did each figure stand for?
    (b) What was the meaning of the figures which were holding flags?
2 After studying the drawings of the dancing men carefully, Holmes found a name and address.
    (a) What was the name?
    (b) What was the address?
3 Holmes had sent a telegram to America.
    (a) Who had Holmes sent the telegram to?
    (b) What had he asked in the telegram?
    (c) What reply had he received?
4 What was the meaning of the final message?
5 Inspector Martin was worried that the criminal might escape. Why was Holmes not worried?

8

1 The sitting-room door opened and a man stepped in.
    (a) What did Holmes do?
    (b) What did Inspector Martin do?
2 What was Abe Slaney's reason for killing Hilton Cubitt?
3 Why did Abe Slaney not believe that Mrs Cubitt was badly injured?
4 Why had Elsie run away from America?
5 What was the reason for the large amount of money in the handbag?
6 Why did Holmes say that the dancing men had finally done some good?

THE RED-HEADED LEAGUE

1

1 When Dr Watson visited Holmes, there was another visitor. What was unusual about this visitor?
2 Mr Wilson showed Watson an advertisement in a newspaper.
    (a) Where was there a vacancy?
    (b) How much was the salary?
    (c) What kind of men should apply?
    (d) Where should they apply?

2

1 Where was Mr Wilson's shop?
2 Who was Vincent Spaulding?
3 There were some unusual things about Vincent Spaulding.
   (a) How much was he willing to work for?
   (b) What was he very interested in?
   (c) Where did he go when he wasn't working?
4 Vincent Spaulding told Mr Wilson that he wished he was a red-headed man. Why?
5 What did Vincent Spaulding tell Mr Wilson which made him very interested in The Red-Headed League?
6 Why did Mr Wilson think it would be easy for him to become a member of The Red-Headed League?

3

1 What did Mr Wilson see in Fleet Street that was so very strange?
2 What was strange about the small man sitting behind the table?
3 Why did the small man pull Mr Wilson's hair?
4 Duncan Ross offered Mr Wilson the job.
   (a) Who was willing to look after Mr Wilson's shop?
   (b) What were the hours of work?
   (c) What was Mr Wilson to do?
   (d) Do you think this was an unusual job? Why?
5 Why was Mr Wilson frightened to leave the office during the hours of work?
6 How did Mr Wilson learn that the job had ended?

4

1 Why did Holmes and Watson begin to laugh?
2 Mr Wilson told Spaulding that the job had ended. What did Spaulding suggest Mr Watson should do?
3 Holmes asked Mr Wilson to describe Spaulding.
   (a) What was unusual about Spaulding's forehead?
   (b) What was unusual about Spaulding's ears?
4 'Watson. Come quickly!' Holmes said to Watson. Where were they going?

5

1 What did Holmes do to the pavement outside Mr Wilson's house in Saxe-Coburg Square?

2 Watson asked Holmes if he had knocked at the door of Mr Wilson's house so that he could have a look at Vincent Spaulding. What was Holmes' reply?

3 What was the difference between the houses in Saxe-Coburg Square and the houses in the street behind the Square?

4 Holmes saw a building in the street behind Saxe-Coburg Square which made him very excited. What building was it?

5 Holmes told Watson that he needed his help.
   (a) When was Watson to come to Holmes' apartment?
   (b) What was Watson to bring with him?

6

1 Who was:
   (a) Peter Jones?
   (b) Mr Merryweather?

2 'Tonight you'll play a more exciting game than cards,' said Holmes to Mr Merryweather.
   (a) What might Mr Merryweather lose?
   (b) What might Jones win?

3 Mr Merryweather told Watson why the criminals were interested in the cellar of the bank. What was the reason?

4 Why were three policemen waiting at the front door of Wilson's shop?

7

1 Watson and the others waited in the cellar, in darkness. Watson suddenly saw a light.
   (a) Where was it coming from?
   (b) What happened to one of the large stones in the floor?

2 'I think my friend has escaped,' said John Clay. What was Mr Jones' reply?

3 Why did Holmes think it had been an interesting case?

1   Why had John Clay and Duncan Ross started The Red-Headed League?
2   Three things made Holmes think that the criminals were digging a tunnel. What were these three things?
3   Why was Holmes sure the criminals would try to rob the cellar under the bank that night?

GLOSSARY

Glossary

1   **private detective** (page 4)
    someone who finds out how a crime happened. Sherlock Holmes is
    not a policeman, he is a private detective. But sometimes he helps
    the police solve crimes or find criminals.

2   **client** (page 4)
    someone who comes to Sherlock Holmes and asks for help.

3   **case** (page 4)
    one of the crimes or mysteries that Holmes tries to solve.

4   **veil** (page 4)
    a thin piece of cloth, worn over a woman's face. (See illustration on
    page 9.)

5   **twins** (page 5)
    two children – brothers or sisters – born at the same time.

6   **private income** (page 6)
    money which a person receives from a bank every year. The person
    who receives the money does not have to do any work.

7   **inherit** (page 6)
    to receive money or a house from someone who has died.

8   **gypsies** (page 6)
    a group of people who do not live in houses and move from one
    place to another.

9   **band** (page 6)
    (a) a group of people who travel together – for example, a band of
    gypsies.
    (b) a piece of cloth worn round the head or neck.

10 **cheetah and baboon** (page 6)
    wild animals from India. A cheetah is a large cat and a baboon is a
    large ape.

11 **fainted** (page 8)
    to feel weak and ill because you are frightened or injured.

12 **handkerchief** (page 10)
    a brightly coloured piece of cloth.

13 **examine** (page 11)
    to look at something very carefully.

14 **will** (page 14)
    a paper written by a person which says what will happen to their
    money and property when that person dies.

15 **ceiling** (page 15)
the part of the room which is over your head.

16 **safe** (page 17)
a strong metal box, where you can keep money or valuables.

17 **noose** (page 17)
a rope twisted round and tied in a circle.

18 **lamp** (page 18)
a light that contains oil or paraffin. When the oil burns it shines brightly.

19 **inn** (page 18)
a place where people stay for the night and have drinks and meals.

20 **sundial** (page 26)
a sundial is a clock which stands outside. It tells the time by the sun. The sun shines on the hands of the sundial and the shadow tells the time.

21 **toolhouse** (page 28)
a building where tools are kept.

22 **telegram** (page 31)
this story happened in 1890. There were no telephones then. The fastest way of sending a message over a distance was by telegram.

23 **committed** – *to commit a crime* (page 33)
when criminals rob a bank, they commit a crime.

24 **investigation** (page 34)
to investigate a crime is to find out how the crime was committed and who the criminals were.

25 **window frame** (page 36)
the wood which is fixed round a window and holds it to the wall.

26 **evidence** (page 37)
anything which helps detectives to understand how a crime was committed and who the criminals were.

27 **crook** (page 41)
another word for criminal.

28 **handcuffs** – *handcuffs on his wrists* (page 43)
handcuffs are a pair of metal rings, joined by a chain. Police put handcuffs on criminals' wrists, so that they cannot easily use their hands.

29 **advertisement** (page 46)
a notice put in a newspaper telling people about jobs, things to see etc.

30 **League** – *Red-Headed League* (page 47)
    a league is a group of people who join together because they are all
    interested in the same thing. A Red-Headed League would be
    people who came together because they all had red hair.
31 *vacancy* (page 47)
    a place for a new worker.
32 *develops* (page 48)
    to develop photographs is to take the film from a camera and make
    pictures. This is done in a dark room like a cellar.
33 **Encyclopaedia Britannica** (page 51)
    a large number of books, like dictionaries, which give information
    about many things.
34 *magnifying glass* (page 59)
    a glass you look through which makes things look larger.

Exercises

The Speckled Band

Multiple Choice

Tick the best answer.

1   Dr Roylott was Helen and Julia's stepfather. What does this mean?
a   ☐ He was no relation to them but their mother asked him to have
    special responsibility for them when they were born.
b   ☐ He was the father of Julia's fiancé.
c   ☑ He married Helen and Julia's mother after they were born.
d   ☐ He was married to Helen and Julia's mother when they were
    born but they divorced soon after.

2   Helen and Julia were twins. What does this mean?
a   ☐ They were sisters of different ages.
b   ☐ They were sisters who were born on the same day.
c   ☐ They were relatives but not sisters.
d   ☐ They had the same mother but different fathers.

DR ROYLOTT'S BEDROOM	JULIA'S BEDROOM

ventilator →

false bell-rope ←

safe

Julia's bed is fixed to the floor

3   The bell-rope was for calling servants. What happened when
    Holmes pulled the rope?
a   ☐ A servant came to the room.
b   ☐ He heard a bell ringing in the kitchen.
c   ☐ The rope fell down because it was only attached to the ceiling.
d   ☐ Nothing happened because it was attached to the ceiling and
    not to a bell.

4 What is a ventilator?

a ☐ A ventilator allows fresh air to come into a room from outside the house.

b ☐ It is like a window that allows light to shine from another room.

c ☐ It is a hole in a wall for speaking to people in another room.

d ☐ It is a small door connecting one room to another.

5 What is a safe?

a ☐ It is a wooden cupboard for keeping clothes.

b ☐ It is a cold storage place, made of metal or plastic, for keeping food.

c ☐ It is a security device that rings an alarm bell when someone enters the house.

d ☐ It is a strong metal box, with a special lock, for keeping valuables.

6 Where did Helen spend the night when Holmes and Dr Watson came to Stoke Moran?

a ☐ In Julia's room.

b ☐ In her own room.

c ☐ In Dr Roylott's room.

d ☐ In the sitting-room.

7 How did Dr Roylott kill Julia?

a ☐ He used Indian magic to make her die in her sleep.

b ☐ He let a baboon and a cheetah into her bedroom.

c ☐ He sent a poisonous snake into her room while she was sleeping.

d ☐ He paid the gypsies to murder her in her bed.

8 How did Dr Roylott die?

a ☐ He was bitten by a poisonous snake.

b ☐ He shot himself.

c ☐ Holmes hit him with a stick.

d ☐ He fell off the chair in his bedroom.

The Dancing Men

Making Sentences

Write questions for the answers.

1 *What were the Dancing Men?*
   The Dancing Men were a kind of secret writing.

2 *What*
   Mr Hilton Cubitt had found a strange message in his garden.

3 *Why*
   He was worried about his wife because she was frightened by the
   Dancing Men message.

4 *Where*
   His wife came from Chicago.

5 *What*
   He had promised not to ask his wife about her past.

6 *Why*
   Mr Cubitt visited Sherlock Holmes again because he had found
   more messages.

7 *Who*
   Holmes sent a telegram to a friend in the New York Police.

8 *What*
   Holmes' telegram said: WHO IS ABE SLANEY?

Comprehension

Holmes found that the secret messages read:
1. AM HERE, ABE SLANEY   2 AT ELRIGES
3. COME ELSIE   4 NEVER
5. ELSIE, PREPARE TO MEET THY GOD

Answer the questions.

1 Where had Abe Slaney come from?

....

2 Why didn't Elsie marry Abe Slaney?

....

....

3 What was Elrige's?

....

4 What did Abe Slaney want Elsie to do?

....

....

5 What was the answer to Holmes' telegram: WHO IS ABE SLANEY?

....

6 Who did Abe Slaney shoot?

....

7 Who shot Elsie Cubitt?

....

8 How did Holmes get Abe Slaney to come back to the Cubitts' house?

....

....

Secret Writing

Messages in secret writing are called *ciphers*. In a simple cipher, each letter of the alphabet is given a sign or substitute.

Look at these signs. This is called the *Hook Line & Sinker Cipher*.

Look at the example.

= Sherlock Holmes

Can you work out what this message means?

The Red-Headed League

Story Outline

Complete the gaps. Use each word in the box once.

suspected   finished   member   outside   ~~shop~~   assistant
interested   cellar   During   help   copying   started
showed   vacancy   offered   advertisement   work
spent   bad   pay   half   rich   upset   knees   explained

Jabez Wilson had a small ¹.......*shop*....... in the City of London.

Business was ²..................... and he was lucky to find an

³..................... who would work for ⁴.....................-pay.

The assistant was very ⁵..................... in photography and

⁶..................... a lot of time in the ⁷..................... of

Jabez Wilson's shop.

The assistant ⁸..................... his employer an

⁹..................... in the newspaper. The assistant

¹⁰..................... that Ezekiah Hopkins was a

¹¹..................... American who had red hair. He left money in

his will to ¹²..................... all red-headed men and he

¹³..................... the Red-Headed League. The Red-Headed

League had a ¹⁴..................... for a new ¹⁵.....................

and Jabez Wilson, who had bright red hair, thought he might be able to

join. He went to an address in Fleet Street and was

¹⁶..................... a job.

He had to [17]................................... in Pope's Court, Fleet Street every day from 10am to 2pm. [18].................................. this time he was not allowed to leave the office. The job involved [19].................................. out an encyclopaedia and the [20]... was four pounds a week.

After two months the job suddenly [21].................................... . Mr Wilson was so [22]................................... that he went to see Sherlock Holmes in Baker Street.

Holmes immediately [23].................................. a crime. He visited Mr Wilson's assistant with Dr Watson, and he was very interested in the [24].................................. of his trousers. Holmes was also interested in what was going on [25].................................. the shop – in particular, behind and below ...

Multiple Choice

Tick the best answer.

1 What is a cellar?
a ☐ It is a room in a shop for selling goods.
b ☐ It is a shop where tailors work.
c ☐ It is a dark place for doing photography.
d ☐ It is a room underneath a building.

2 What was behind Jabez Wilson's shop?
a ☐ A park.
b ☐ A bank.
c ☐ A wall.
d ☐ A courtyard.

3 Why did John Clay think of starting The Red-Headed League?

a ☐ Because Mr Wilson had the same colour hair as his friend.

b ☐ Because he wanted to help people with red hair.

c ☐ Because he had red hair himself.

d ☐ Because he didn't like people with red hair.

4 What were the criminals doing while Jabez Wilson was working for the Red-Headed League?

a ☐ They were developing photographs in the cellar.

b ☐ They were learning how to run Mr Wilson's business.

c ☐ They drank tea and ate biscuits all day.

d ☐ They were digging a tunnel from the cellar to the bank.

5 Who was Vincent Spaulding?

a ☐ A dangerous criminal.

b ☐ A shop assistant who liked photography.

c ☐ A member of The Red-Headed League.

d ☐ A builder.

6 What did the notice THE RED-HEADED LEAGUE IS FINISHED mean to Holmes?

a ☐ It meant that the league had run out of money.

b ☐ It meant that there were no more red-headed men.

c ☐ It meant that Jabez Wilson did not have a job.

d ☐ It meant that the criminals had finished the tunnel.

7 How did Holmes know that the cellar was at the back of the house?

a ☐ He knocked on the pavement in front of the house with his stick.

b ☐ He had been to the house before.

c ☐ He went into the house while Spaulding was out.

d ☐ He saw it through a window at the back of the house.

Words From the Stories

H	C	C	C	R	O	O	K	D	E	X
I	E	C	L	H	M	U	P	E	V	L
L	I	L	S	I	L	P	B	T	I	A
H	L	E	C	A	E	L	J	E	D	M
S	I	A	J	A	F	N	D	C	E	P
R	N	G	G	P	S	E	T	T	N	P
J	G	U	X	N	I	E	P	I	C	F
T	O	E	S	A	M	V	E	V	E	X
I	N	H	E	R	I	T	Y	E	Z	E
V	E	T	E	L	E	G	R	A	M	T
B	T	B	R	V	A	C	A	N	C	Y

Find words in the square with the meanings below. The numbers in brackets show the number of letters in each word.

1 one of the crimes or mysteries that Holmes solves (4) ....*CASE*..........
2 the part of the room which is over your head (7) ....
3 someone who comes to Holmes and asks for help (6) ....
4 a slang word for a criminal (5) ....
5 a person who investigates crimes (9) ....
6 proof of who committed a crime (8) ....
7 to receive money or property from
someone who has died (7) ....
8 a light that burns oil or paraffin (4) ....
9 a group of people who join together
because of a common interest (6) ....
10 a strong metal box for keeping money
and valuables (4) ....
11 a message sent by telegraph (8) ....
12 a position or place that is free or unoccupied (7) ....

Published by Macmillan Heinemann ELT
Between Towns Road, Oxford OX4 3PP
Macmillan Heinemann ELT is an imprint of
Macmillan Publishers Limited
Companies and representatives throughout the world
Heinemann is a registered trademark of Harcourt Education, used under licence.

ISBN 978-0-230-03048-0
ISBN 978-1-4050-7680-7 (with CD edition)

This retold version by Anne Collins for Macmillan Readers
First published 1986
Text © Anne Collins 1986, 1992, 1998, 2002, 2005
Design and illustration © Macmillan Publishers Limited 2002, 2005

This edition first published 2005

Illustrated by Kay Dixey
Original cover template design by Jackie Hill
Cover photography by Corbis/Bob Krist

Printed in Thailand

with CD edition

2009 2008 2007
10 9 8 7

without CD edition

2009 2008 2007
4 3 2 1